The Illuminutty

New World Disorder

By

Rev Nathon Dees

The Life and Times of Texas Guitar legend Nathon Dees

Ok so I survived Book one and Book Two and now I'm back in Costa Rica safe and sound as an intellectual refuge. I have managed to clear my mind and focus more clearly on my future. Through introspection and self evaluation I was able to see through the bad programming and come to a higher revelation of the truth. Lies and misconceptions had been taught to me in American society as Gospel truths my entire life. When these concepts of the constructs of reality were met with certain realisms they caused Cognitive Dissonance with the primary operating psychological program and shorted me out. It is like putting a person in a round room and telling them to sit in the corner.

It was no longer a Matter of Belief but more of a matter of understanding and Gnosis through higher Consciousness. I had to lay out every construct of my primary operating command in such a way as to monitor the cause and effect of each primary beliefs function and end result. After doing so and reorganizing my belief system by inventorying and evaluating clearly the things that I CHOSE to believe I was able to break free from the Ego identity that had been created by Religion and Society in the United States of Confusion.

Chapter One

Video Gaming Theory

My son Aaron and my daughter Natolie are both Gamers and as a Father I have spent countless hours watching them kill aliens, save planets, overtake war zones in alternate realities and learn to overcome obstacles and achieve Mastery. I have an application theory that I call "Mastery Application" everyone is always recreating the wheel. Once you achieve mastery in one art you immediately apply that same exact level of expertise to every area of your life. So here is where the theory applies.

sense at all. In fact it is almost impossible to believe. You see in the Military and Marshall arts when we recognize a Rank of another branch of Service or fighting style and we still honor their mastery and treat them as equals, well you young people can create a perfect world on a screen and can't tie your own shoes in reality and this is absolute insanity! You are not applying the Mastery that you have already achieved. "But that guy went to school for that" Big Fucking deal you mindless automaton, the guy that invented it DID NOT GO TO SCHOOL FOR IT, HE JUST DID IT!!!!!!GET IT! He just Did It!

My point is, if you can create and manipulate a perfect life for yourself on Simms then why does your real life suck? It is because you fail to apply the lessons that you have learned in the Video reality to the Functioning Reality. It's like saying "Oh I can't Drive a FORD I was only taught to drive a Chevy. I can't Play Bass I was only taught to play guitar. I can't fly a plane of surf or skate or shoot or skate board in real life I can only do it on a video game. I call Bullshit! If the basic skills needed to achieve a Task are present in a Video reality then they are present in the Functioning reality. It's the same Fucking Brain; it is the same Fucking Game!

When one meditates on nothing and removes oneself from one's self you can then throw up your internal video monitor and evaluate who exactly is playing your avatar in this three Dimensional reality Game. Understand that in the format of an RPG you constantly check your health, Your Spells, Your Knowledge, and you inventory what you truly need to accomplish your task. You would never knowingly nor willingly choose destructive actions that would be detrimental to the success of the mission or subtract from you overall performance and placement ranking. So why then in Life are we Complete Fucktards that have absolutely no Fucking idea what is going on when in an alternate holographic reality we are Gods!

So I'm like "Son, Life is coming against you and you are taking it pretty hard. You have made some incorrect decisions and you are suffering from the cause and effect of your decisions. You feel as if everything is against you and to every positive effort there is an equal and opposite effort against you. Well that's because it is!!!! In fact it is the Ebb and flow of Conscious reality and the very struggle to find balance within.

So you are a Jedi Star Fleet Commander and a Four Star General in Knights of the New Republic and Medal of Honor but in the Third Dimensional Holographic Reality you are living on your friends couch and can't get a job because you have no car etc etc etc. This makes absolutely no Fucking

The game is called "Evolutionary Ascension" and you are the Avatar. You are a three dimensional Psychotronic Humanoid Borg on a Planetary Omniversity and you must graduate or you will be recycled infinitely as an unascended gaming character in the Holographic matrix until you Wake up Evolve and Ascend. Unfortunately Your DNA has been modified and you have to unlock your condones to access your akasha records so you are Stupid and your Karma Score Card keeps following you from incarnation to incarnation until you get it right.

Wow I just explained the concept of cyclic reality in one paragraph. All of the Eastern, Middle East, Mesa American, Inuit, Gaelic, Pictic, Egyptian, Zoroaster, and on and on and on all the way back to ancient Samaria believed and practiced this Philosophy until the dawning of the age of Materialism and the Birth of Organized religion. Akhenaton was sent to destroy religion and bring truth, Hermes was sent to do it, Dioneses was sent to do it, Pythagoras was sent to do it, Horus was sent to do it, Krishna was sent to do it, Thoth was sent to do it, Enoch was sent to do it, Quetzucatal was sent to do it Yeshua "Jesus Christ" was sent to do it and now I had been incarnated in this Eon to do it again.

Chapter Two

Programmed on a Foundation of Lies

The problem with child rearing inside the American societal culture such as the one that I was raised in is a blurring of the truth while programming the foundations that the child lives on. When we don't clearly define what is fact, what is fiction, and what is faith so we establish a foundation of misinformation, half truths and Folklore. Santa Clause, The Easter Bunny, and Jesus all on the same plain of existence with Satan getting his own Holiday Halloween when he was in direct opposition to Jesus. Santa Clause and the Easter Bunny getting Billing over the Christ? Blowing the young and impressionable minds of children with Lies and Myths for the purpose of what? Propagating societal lies for fun? Teaching you children that it is OK to lie if it is tradition? Forcing the older children to lie to the younger children to further propagate more lies? This is absolute Fucking insanity and is not only Cruel to children but it establishes a standard of no moral absolutes in the name of celebrating moral absolutes and programs your children to believe in Historical mythical figures as Gods and Deities for the purpose of entertainment only to eventually learn that it was a lie but yet hold true to the religious iconic idolatry that the icons represent. This is where the foundation for theological cognitive dissonance is established.

I never once did any of this and I never lied to my children because it was popular. I explained clearly the difference between folk lore and much and I also explained to my children that the other parents lacked integrity and lie to their children but I did not want to do that. We had no Santa, we did not celebrate Halloween, and we never celebrated Easter. This made me a bad parent? I was protecting the integrity of the relationship that I had with my Kids as a source of accurate information and truth!

Chapter Three

The Book of N8

1. In the Beginning was the end and the end was the beginning thereof.

2	What is now was then and what was then will be now again in the Cyclic flow of consciousness.

3	The beginning is the end of that which was before it.

4	This is the Ubiquitous Flow of conscious Reality as you perceive it an ever evolving always improving program in a cosmic quest for completion only to perpetually reproduce for infinity.

5   A Holographic 3D Reality constructed and controlled by the sentient Conscious Observation of other Intelligible Humans in agreement.

6   A plastic shapeable reality that you can control to some extent by exercising ones will and determination to Rise Above the simplicity of Normality and Create a Better World to live in for the Whole by raising Awareness and Consciousness to the Masses instead of educational Mind Control in an Slave Society of mindless automatons.

Chapter Four

Pull Your Head Out

This is a definitive guide to pulling your head out of your ass and getting a clue.

First things first. Stop Bullshitting yourself! If you are fucked up you damn well know it so just stop lying to yourself and everyone else. Stop comparing yourself to other people that are more Fucked up than you are and Stop Blaming other people for you being Fucked up. Pinch, Wipe, Flush and Get over it.

Now that we have decided to get real and actually evaluate how and why we became Fucked up in the first place and correct the programming errors that brought us to this place.

Chapter Five

Troubleshooting 101

Self Diagnosis. Use introspection and some meditation to analyze your condition and answer your own questions intelligently and with objectivity like you actually have a clue and you know right from wrong because you do!

Stop playing dumb ass like some immature little kid that pretends to not know that wrong actions and wrong behavior lead to bad results. If you don't have a Clue Get One! Pull your fucking head out of your ass and find out what is right and wrong from some one that has their shit together at any level of life that is better than yours!

Start filing your mind with good information and stop hanging around with STUPID PEOPLE that do STUPID SHIT!

Separate yourself from STUPID PEOPLE that do STUPID THINGS and start hanging out with SMART PEOPLE that are doing POSSATIVE THINGS! So if you're at a Metal bar and your old friend says "Hey lets Smoke this Meth and Jump in the Mosh PITT" and your new friend looks at your like "WTF" go with the Smart Guy! You have just pulled your head out of your ass and Got a Clue at that very moment and the Next time you might get to be the Smart Friend!

Chapter Six

More Rambling

So is my Narcissism not the equal and opposite reaction to your stupidity? Is there something wrong with me because I can see what's wrong with everything? Why can't they see the flaws in the constructs of the values of religion and society? Why would a world of mindless automatons have a say in the future of mankind or the planet? Why would it not make perfect since to eliminate the week and feeble minded so that the race can flourish? What kind of selfishness would allow everyone to suffer because of the actions of the Dumb Masses? Is this social, ethnic and religious cleansing not the very hope of all religion? Only by eliminating the Bad seed can the good seed flourish and there are simply too many average or normal people to sustain and a purging and cleansing is inevitable and unavoidable. Mankind is a fungus to the Earth that has grown out of control and outlived its usefulness to the good of the whole and nature itself will find balance one way or another.

This is just another cycle in the planets evolution and has taken place many times with many beings and cultures. The masking of truth to enslave the dumb Masses has reached its critical mass but the intrinsic thinking ability of the dumb masses is so low that they still cannot evaluate the truth that is now being presented because it violates the core of their educational and religious programming. One will never be able to grasp the reality of Truth while clinging to superstitions, myths and religious ideologies when met with the indisputable truth that their world as they know it is coming to an end. The sooner the Better!

CHAPTER 7

New World Disorder

So I'm researching and researching trying to figure something out that's concrete. I am now an expert as it were on Atlantis, Lumeria, Mu, Ancient Mesopotamia, Egypt, Samaria, Mesoamerica, etc etc. I've studied every ancient religious text that I could get my hands on searching for any higher truth or in fact any truth at all by this point. The one thing that I knew for sure was that there was a grand conspiracy of misinformation out there and truths were only found deep beyond the surface of things.

Meanwhile back in the present all of the things I'm learning about the past all tie into the present and center around two families or blood lines. A brother, a half brother and a sister.

Over and over again. Different names same story, same time lines, same results. A power struggle between two opposing forces for the rule of Earth. Yet none of it was real. Everything was a type and everything was holistic in an ever occurring infinite spiral of realities. Every Star was a god and every element a spirit and it was all a master program of seven basic harmonic tones. Frequency resonance creating the perceptions of a three dimensional holographic reality held together only by sentient consciousness and consciousness was failing rapidly on this planet.

All of the evidences showed that an elite few were controlling the World to some extent but yet it had to be done. Everything looked as if they were preparing for alien invasion and genocide while at the same time everything that they were doing would be absolutely necessary for maintain control and preserving the balance of the planet.

Those that know, know and those that do not know do not know. All knowledge is transient and in the very fiber of your DNA. There is nothing that is not known. There is only that that has not yet been revealed or understood but there is no thing that has not yet been conceived already in the prime directive of the program.

It is our task or goal as it were to wake up in this lifetime and come to the reality of what truly is and find balance with ourselves that we may achieve personal evolution and overcome this three dimensional existence and move on to a higher dimensional plane. What is , is.

Back to the story at hand.

The Zionist banksters and the and the Royal families "NATO" are preparing to take over the Earth it would seem by destroying all religion and religious groups and forming a one world government through marshal law and genocide. The whole thing was playing out like some bad Hollywood movie or a high tech video game. The U.S. had become a slave state with a puppet government controlled by the families. Those that were in power were going to exterminate the human cattle and start over. As evil and sinister as it all seemed it all made a great deal of since to me. To a higher dimensional being we would be no different than any other lower life form is to us. The same prejudices that we show and experience over our own opinions towards certain life would be expressed by any other life form than ourselves. A dog is a dog unless it's your dog.

If you did know what was going to happen and you had a chance of saving the best of the best you would do so. If you were in power and you truly understood the events to come and had the ability to survive and reconstruct by whatever means necessary then you would do so. It just makes since.

Compassion is not a necessary trait for a surviving species. The substandard human species created on this planet by mistake must be eliminated and the quarantine lifted off of this planet for cosmic equilibrium to be achieved. It is no different than bad seed in your garden or a mutt dog breeding with your prize show dog. The bad DNA must be eradicated for the survival of the overall race. Or let's put it this way. It's not going to survive anyway in a post apocalyptic world.

They had discovered a way for them to live forever as it were by using self replicating Nanotechnology and creating an advanced humanoid Borg that was one with artificial intelligence. They no longer needed humans to do their bidding for them on Earth so they were going to exterminate them. What they did not realize in their selfish quest for eternity was that what they were creating already existed and they were it. We are the program. We are the self replicating life form and the infinite knowledge is available to those of a pure heart. It is appointed unto a man to live and die ass all things have a cycle. Nature shall run its course and it will determine who survives. What is , is.

They have created their modern Tower of Babble and the Aeons and Archons will once again set all things in order.

Haughty and high minded art thou Oh man that would try and reach the heavens and dethrone The God's if it were possible.

Eternity is found within one's own heart. It is the Cosmic Bliss of Love and nothing else. Only The Arc of Love can bend light frequency into reality. True life is consciousness as to be unconscious is to be void of life in this third dimensional reality. Your only existence is that that is held within your own perceptions of reality in this holographic dream World. Don't believe anything just be, for what is, is and what is not is not. It is truly your own perception of what is that creates the constructs of your own personal reality. All that shall be shall be as it was in the beginning that it shall be again. The cycle must continue and evolution of the species must occur. http://youtu.be/EIUN-vUuqcw

They had created an insane society of impossible constructs that enslaved people into a realm of cognitive dissonance. By reconstructing the harmonic grid to one of imbalance they could prevent true bliss and understanding thereby preventing the masses to ever achieve inner peace or higher revelation. Feeding off of the suffering of the masses while they obtain great hordes of wealth for themselves until the time of the harvest just like cattle farmers fattening up a herd for slaughter. It was dinner time and their god's were returning to Earth for the harvest one more time.

So would end another cycle and a new and better world would begin.

It all seemed to have the same ending no matter how it played out. It would be a new beginning for someone, one way or another. There must be an end for a beginning to occur in every construct of reality.

Chapter 8

Comet ISON and the Great Deception

It is Oct of 2013 and as the Comet ISON quickly approaches Earth the U.S. Government has shut down in an effort to destroy the economy and declare Marshall Law on the People of the United States. FEMA region three is prepared for lock down and the East Coast is getting hit with fireballs daily now. All of the Government websites have been shut down including NASA and there is no information about any of this on the news. ISON already arced electrically with Mars and caused it to have a Coma and go Comet and everyone on the Earth is just too fucking stupid to realize the truth of what was really going on. Fukashima Japan is a

fucking nuclear disaster and Cyclones were distributing radiation all over the world. Solar flares are increasing daily and the power grid on Earth would be knocked out any day now. You can almost time the solar flares and the Earth quakes that follow daily now. The great change is upon us and a New World Order is eminent but the one question still remained, who would be in control. I am predicting the return of the God's and the Judgment of the leaders of the Earth followed by a Millennium of peace on Earth. Let's just sit back and see what really happens.

I stole this Document and I can't speak for it's validity but I highly recommend that you give it a glance. N8

Silent Weapons for Quiet Wars, An Introduction Programming Manual was uncovered quite by accident on July 7, 1986 when an employee of Boeing Aircraft Co. purchased a surplus IBM copier for scrap parts at a sale, and discovered inside details of a plan, hatched in the embryonic days of the "Cold War" which called for control of the masses through manipulation of industry, peoples' pastimes, education and political leanings. It called for a quiet revolution, putting brother against brother, and diverting the public's attention from what is really going on.
The document you are about to read is real. It is reprinted in its virgin form, with diagrams, as a touch of reality.

Table of Contents

The following document, dated May 1979, was found on July 7, 1986, in an IBM copier that had been purchased at a surplus sale.

TOP SECRET

Silent Weapons for Quiet Wars

Operations Research Technical Manual TM-SW7905.1

Welcome Aboard

This publication marks the 25th anniversary of the Third World War, called the "Quiet War", being conducted using subjective biological warfare, fought with "silent weapons."

This book contains an introductory description of this war, its strategies, and its weaponry.

May 1979 #74-1120

Security

It is patently impossible to discuss social engineering or the automation of a society, i.e., the engineering of social automation systems (silent weapons) on a national or worldwide scale without implying extensive objectives of social control and destruction of human life, i.e., slavery and genocide.

This manual is in itself an analog declaration of intent. Such a writing must be secured from public scrutiny. Otherwise, it might be recognized as a technically formal declaration of domestic war. Furthermore, whenever any person or group of persons in a position of great power and without full knowledge and consent of the public, uses such knowledge and methodologies for economic conquest – it must be understood that a state of domestic warfare exists between said person or group of persons and the public.

The solution of today's problems requires an approach which is ruthlessly candid, with no agonizing over religious, moral or cultural values.

You have qualified for this project because of your ability to look at human society with cold objectivity, and yet analyze and discuss your observations and conclusions with others of similar intellectual capacity without the loss of discretion or humility. Such virtues are exercised in your own best interest. Do not deviate from them.

Historical Introduction

Silent weapon technology has evolved from *Operations Research* (O.R.), a strategic and tactical methodology developed under the Military Management in England during World War II. The original purpose of Operations Research was to study the strategic and tactical problems of air and land defense with the objective of effective use of limited military resources against foreign enemies (i.e., logistics).

It was soon recognized by those in positions of power that the same methods might be useful for totally controlling a society. But better tools were necessary.

Social engineering (the analysis and automation of a society) requires the correlation of great amounts of constantly changing economic information (data), so a high-speed computerized data-processing system was necessary which could race ahead of the society and predict when society would arrive for capitulation.

Relay computers were to slow, but the electronic computer, invented in 1946 by J. Presper Eckert and John W. Mauchly, filled the bill.

The next breakthrough was the development of the *simplex method* of linear programming in 1947 by the mathematician George B. Dantzig.

Then in 1948, the transistor, invented by J. Bardeen, W.H. Brattain, and W. Shockley, promised great expansion of the computer field by reducing space and power requirements.

With these three inventions under their direction, those in positions of power strongly suspected that it was possible for them to control the whole world with the push of a button.

Immediately, the Rockefeller Foundation got in on the ground floor by making a four-year grant to Harvard College, funding the *Harvard Economic Research Project* for the study of the structure of the American Economy. One year later, in 1949, The United States Air Force joined in.

In 1952 the grant period terminated, and a high-level meeting of the Elite was held to determine the next phase of social operations research. The Harvard project had been very fruitful, as is borne out by the publication of some of its results in 1953 suggesting the feasibility of economic (social) engineering. (*Studies in the Structure of the American Economy* - copyright 1953 by Wassily Leontief, International Science Press Inc., White Plains, New York).

Engineered in the last half of the decade of the 1940's, the new Quiet War machine stood, so to speak, in sparkling gold-plated hardware on the showroom floor by 1954.

With the creation of the *maser* in 1954, the promise of unlocking unlimited sources of fusion atomic energy from the heavy hydrogen in sea water and the consequent availability of unlimited social power was a possibility only decades away.

The combination was irresistible.

The Quiet War was quietly declared by the International Elite at a meeting held in 1954.

Although the silent weapons system was nearly exposed 13 years later, the evolution of the new weapon-system has never suffered any major setbacks.

This volume marks the 25th anniversary of the beginning of the Quiet War. Already this domestic war has had many victories on many fronts throughout the world.

Political Introduction

In 1954 it was well recognized by those in positions of authority that it was only a matter of time, only a few decades, before the general public would be able to grasp and upset the cradle of power, for the very elements of the new silent-weapon technology were as accessible for a public utopia as they were for providing a private utopia.

The issue of primary concern, that of dominance, revolved around the subject of the energy sciences.

Energy

Energy is recognized as the key to all activity on earth. Natural science is the study of the sources and control of natural energy, and social science, theoretically expressed as economics, is the study of the sources and control of social energy. Both are bookkeeping systems: mathematics. Therefore, mathematics is the primary energy science. And the bookkeeper can be king if the public can be kept ignorant of the methodology of the bookkeeping.

All science is merely a means to an end. The means is knowledge. The end is control. Beyond this remains only one issue: Who will be the beneficiary?

In 1954 this was the issue of primary concern. Although the so-called "moral issues" were raised, in view of the law of natural selection it was agreed that a nation or world of people who will not use their intelligence are no better than animals who do not have intelligence. Such people are beasts of burden and steaks on the table by choice and consent.

Consequently, in the interest of future world order, peace, and tranquillity, it was decided to privately wage a quiet war against the American public with an ultimate objective of permanently shifting the natural and social energy (wealth) of the undisciplined and irresponsible many into the hands of the self-disciplined, responsible, and worthy few.

In order to implement this objective, it was necessary to create, secure, and apply new weapons which, as it turned out, were a class of weapons so subtle and sophisticated in their principle of operation and public appearance as to earn for themselves the name "silent weapons."

In conclusion, the objective of economic research, as conducted by the magnates of capital (banking) and the industries of commodities (goods) and services, is the establishment of an economy which is totally predictable and manipulatable.

In order to achieve a totally predictable economy, the low-class elements of society must be brought under total control, i.e., must be housebroken, trained, and assigned a yoke and long-term social duties from a very early age, before they have an opportunity to question the propriety of the matter. In order to achieve such conformity, the lower-class family unit must be disintegrated by a process of increasing preoccupation of the parents and the establishment of government-operated day-care centers for the occupationally orphaned children.

The quality of education given to the lower class must be of the poorest sort, so that the moat of ignorance isolating the inferior class from the superior class is and remains incomprehensible to the inferior class. With such an initial handicap, even bright lower class individuals have little if any hope of extricating themselves from their assigned lot in life. This form of slavery is essential to maintain some measure of social order, peace, and tranquillity for the ruling upper class.

Descriptive Introduction of the Silent Weapon

Everything that is expected from an ordinary weapon is expected from a silent weapon by its creators, but only in its own manner of functioning.

It shoots situations, instead of bullets; propelled by data processing, instead of chemical reaction (explosion); originating from bits of data, instead of grains of gunpowder; from a computer, instead of a gun; operated by a computer programmer, instead of a marksman; under the orders of a banking magnate, instead of a military general.

It makes no obvious explosive noises, causes no obvious physical or mental injuries, and does not obviously interfere with anyone's daily social life. Yet it makes an unmistakable "noise," causes unmistakable physical and mental damage, and unmistakably interferes with the daily social life, i.e., unmistakable to a trained observer, one who knows what to look for.

The public cannot comprehend this weapon, and therefore cannot believe that they are being attacked and subdued by a weapon.

The public might instinctively feel that something is wrong, but that is because of the technical nature of the silent weapon, they cannot express their feeling in a rational way, or handle the problem with intelligence. Therefore, they do not know how to cry for help, and do not know how to associate with others to defend themselves against it.

When a silent weapon is applied gradually, the public adjusts/adapts to its presence and learns to tolerate its encroachment on their lives until the pressure (psychological via economic) becomes too great and they crack up.

Therefore, the silent weapon is a type of biological warfare. It attacks the vitality, options, and mobility of the individuals of a society by knowing, understanding, manipulating, and attacking their sources of natural and social energy, and their physical, mental, and emotional strengths and weaknesses.

Theoretical Introduction

Give me control over a nation's currency, and I care not who makes its laws.– Mayer Amschel Rothschild, 1743 – 1812)

Today's silent weapons technology is an outgrowth of a simple idea discovered, succinctly expressed, and effectively applied by the quoted *Mr. Mayer Amschel Rothschild*. Mr. Rothschild discovered the missing passive component of economic theory known as economic inductance. He, of course, did not think of his discovery in these 20th-century terms, and, to be sure, mathematical analysis had to wait for the Second Industrial Revolution, the rise of the theory of mechanics and electronics, and finally, the invention of the electronic computer before it could be effectively applied in the control of the world economy.

General Energy Concepts

In the study of energy systems, there always appears three elementary concepts. These are potential energy, kinetic energy, and energy dissipation. And corresponding to these concepts, there are three idealized, essentially pure physical counterparts called passive components.

1. In the science of physical mechanics, the phenomenon of *potential energy* is associated with a physical property called elasticity or stiffness, and can be represented by a stretched spring.In electronic science, potential energy is stored in a capacitor instead of a spring. This property is called capacitance instead of elasticity or stiffness.
2. In the science of physical mechanics, the phenomenon of *kinetic energy* is associated with a physical property called inertia or mass, and can be represented by a mass or a flywheel in motion.In electronic science, kinetic energy is stored in an inductor (in a magnetic field) instead of a mass. This property is called inductance instead of inertia.
3. In the science of physical mechanics, the phenomenon of *energy dissipation* is associated with a physical property called friction or resistance, and can be represented by a dashpot or other device which converts energy into heat.In electronic science, dissipation of energy is performed by an element called either a resistor or a conductor, the term "resistor" being the one generally used to describe a more ideal device (e.g., wire) employed to convey electronic energy efficiently from one location to another. The property of a resistance or conductor is measured as either resistance or conductance reciprocals.

In economics these three energy concepts are associated with:

1. Economic Capacitance - Capital (money, stock/inventory, investments in buildings and durables, etc.)
2. Economic Conductance - Goods (production flow coefficients)
3. Economic Inductance - Services (the influence of the population of industry on output)

All of the mathematical theory developed in the study of one energy system (e.g., mechanics, electronics, etc.) can be immediately applied in the study of any other energy system (e.g., economics).

Mr. Rothchild's Energy Discovery

What Mr. Rothschild had discovered was the basic principle of power, influence, and control over people as applied to economics. That principle is "when you assume the appearance of power, people soon give it to you."

Mr. Rothschild had discovered that currency or deposit loan accounts had the required appearance of power that could be used to induce people (inductance, with people corresponding to a magnetic field) into surrendering their real wealth in exchange for a promise of greater wealth (instead of real compensation). They would put up real collateral in exchange for a loan of promissory notes. Mr. Rothschild found that he could issue more notes than he had backing for, so long as he had someone's stock of gold as a persuader to show his customers.

Mr. Rothschild loaned his promissory notes to individual and to governments. These would create overconfidence. Then he would make money scarce, tighten control of the system, and collect the collateral through the obligation of contracts. The cycle was then repeated. These pressures could be used to ignite a war. Then he would control the availability of currency to determine who would win the war. That government which agreed to give him control of its economic system got his support.

Collection of debts was guaranteed by economic aid to the enemy of the debtor. The profit derived from this economic methodology mad Mr. Rothschild all the more able to expand his wealth. He found that the public greed would allow currency to be printed by government order beyond the limits (inflation) of backing in precious metal or the production of goods and services.

Apparent Capital as "Paper" Inductor

In this structure, credit, presented as a pure element called "currency," has the appearance of capital, but is in effect negative capital. Hence, it has the appearance of service, but is in fact, indebtedness or debt. It is therefore an economic inductance instead of an economic capacitance, and if balanced in no other way, will be balanced by the negation of population (war, genocide). The total goods and services represent real capital called the gross national product, and currency may be printed up to this level and still represent economic capacitance; but currency printed beyond this level is subtractive, represents the introduction of economic inductance, and constitutes notes of indebtedness.

War is therefore the balancing of the system by killing the true creditors (the public which we have taught to exchange true value for inflated currency) and falling back on whatever is left of the resources of nature and regeneration of those resources.

Mr. Rothschild had discovered that currency gave him the power to rearrange the economic structure to his own advantage, to shift economic inductance to those economic positions which would encourage the greatest economic instability and oscillation.

The final key to economic control had to wait until there was sufficient data and high-speed computing equipment to keep close watch on the economic oscillations created by price shocking and excess paper energy credits – paper inductance/inflation.

Breakthrough

The aviation field provided the greatest evolution in economic engineering by way of the mathematical theory of shock testing. In this process, a projectile is fired from an airframe on the ground and the impulse of the recoil is monitored by vibration transducers connected to the airframe and wired to chart recorders.

By studying the echoes or reflections of the recoil impulse in the airframe, it is possible to discover critical vibrations in the structure of the airframe which either vibrations of the engine or *aeolian vibrations* of the wings, or a combination of the two, might reinforce resulting in a resonant self-destruction of the airframe in flight as an aircraft. From the standpoint of engineering, this means that the strengths and weaknesses of the structure of the airframe in terms of vibrational energy can be discovered and manipulated.

Application in Economics

To use this method of airframe shock testing in economic engineering, the prices of commodities are shocked, and the public consumer reaction is monitored. The resulting echoes of the economic shock are interpreted theoretically by computers and the psycho-economic structure of the economy is thus discovered. It is by this process that *partial differential and difference matrices* are discovered that define the family household and make possible its evaluation as an economic industry (dissipative consumer structure).

Then the response of the household to future shocks can be predicted and manipulated, and society becomes a well-regulated animal with its reins under the control of a sophisticated computer-regulated social energy bookkeeping system.

Eventually every individual element of the structure comes under computer control through a knowledge of personal preferences, such knowledge guaranteed by computer association of consumer preferences (universal product code, UPC; zebra-striped pricing codes on packages) with identified consumers (identified via association with the use of a credit card and later a permanent "tattooed" body number invisible under normal ambient illumination).

Summary

Economics is only a social extension of a natural energy system. It, also, has its three passive components. Because of the distribution of wealth and the lack of communication and lack of data, this field has been the last energy field for which a knowledge of these three passive components has been developed.

Since energy is the key to all activity on the face of the earth, it follows that in order to attain a monopoly of energy, raw materials, goods, and services and to establixh a world system of slave labor, it is necessary to have a first strike capability in the field of economics. In order to maintain our position, it is necessary that we have absolute first knowledge of the science of control over all economic factors and the first experience at engineering the world economy.

In order to achieve such sovereignty, we must at least achieve this one end: that the public will not make either the logical or mathematical connection between economics and the other energy sciences or learn to apply such knowledge.

This is becoming increasingly difficult to control because more and more businesses are making demands upon their computer programmers to create and apply mathematical models for the management of those businesses.

It is only a matter of time before the new breed of private programmer/economists will catch on to the far reaching implications of the work begun at Harvard in 1948. The speed with which they can communicate their warning to the public will largely depend upon how effective we have been at controlling the media, subverting education, and keeping the public distracted with matters of no real importance.

The Economic Model

Economics, as a social energy science has as a first objective the description of the complex way in which any given unit of resources is used to satisfy some economic want. (Leontief Matrix). This first objective, when it is extended to get the most product from the least or limited resources, comprises that objective of general military and industrial logistics known as Operations Research. (See simplex method of linear programming.)

The *Harvard Economic Research Project* (1948-) was an extension of World War II *Operations Research*. Its purpose was to discover the science of controlling an economy: at first the American economy, and then the world economy. It was felt that with sufficient mathematical foundation and data, it would be nearly as easy to predict and control the trend of an economy as to predict and control the trajectory of a projectile. Such has proven to be the case. Moreover, the economy has been transformed into a guided missile on target.

The immediate aim of the Harvard project was to discover the economic structure, what forces change that structure, how the behavior of the structure can be predicted, and how it can be manipulated. What was needed was a well-organized knowledge of the mathematical structures and interrelationships of investment, production, distribution, and consumption.

To make a short story of it all, it was discovered that an economy obeyed the same laws as electricity and that all of the mathematical theory and practical and computer know-how developed for the electronic field could be directly applied in the study of economics. This discovery was not openly declared, and its more subtle implications were and are kept a closely guarded secret, for example that in an economic model, human life is measured in dollars, and that the electric spark generated when opening a switch connected to an active inductor is mathematically analogous to the initiation of war.

The greatest hurdle which theoretical economists faced was the accurate description of the household as an industry. This is a challenge because consumer purchases are a matter of choice which in turn is influenced by income, price, and other economic factors.

This hurdle was cleared in an indirect and statistically approximate way by an application of shock testing to determine the current characteristics, called current technical coefficients, of a household industry

Finally, because problems in theoretical electronics can be translated very easily into problems of theoretical electronics, and the solution translated back again, it follows that only a book of language translation and concept definition needed to be written for economics. The remainder could be gotten from standard works on mathematics and electronics. This makes the publication of books on advanced economics unnecessary, and greatly simplifies project security.

Industrial Diagrams

An ideal industry is defined as a device which receives value from other industries in several forms and converts them into one specific product for sales and distribution to other industries. It has several inputs and one output. What the public normally thinks of as one industry is really an industrial complex, where several industries under one roof produce one or more products.

A pure (single output) industry can be represented oversimply by a circuit block as follows:

The flow of product from industry #1 (supply) to industry #2 (demand) is denoted by 112. The total flow out of industry "K" is denoted by Ik (sales, etc.).

A three industry network can be diagrammed as follows:

A node is a symbol of collection and distribution of flow. Node #3 receives from industry #3 and distributes to industries #1 and #3. If industry #3 manufactures chairs, then a flow from industry #3 back to industry #3 simply indicates that industry #3 is using part of its own output product, for example, as office furniture. Therefore the flow may be summarized by the equations:

Three Industrial Classes

Industries fall into three categories or classes by type of output:

1. Class #1 – Capital (resources)
2. Class #2 – Goods (commodities or use – dissipative)
3. Class #3 – Services (action of population)

- Class #1 industries exist at three levels:
  1. Nature – sources of energy and raw materials.
  2. Government – printing of currency equal to the gross national product (GNP), and extension of currency in excess of GNP.
  3. Banking – loaning of money for interest, and extension (inflation/counterfeiting) of economic value through the deposit loan accounts.
- Class #2 industries exist as producers of tangible or consumer (dissipated) products. This sort of activity is usually recognized and labeled by the public as "industry."
- Class #3 industries are those which have service rather than a tangible product as their output. These industries are called (1) households, and (2) governments. Their output is human activity of a mechanical sort, and their basis is population.

Aggregation
The whole economic system can be represented by a three-industry model if one allows the names of the outputs to be (1) capital, (2) goods, and (3) services. The problem with this representation is that it would not show the influence, say, the textile industry on the ferrous metal industry. This is because both the textile industry and the ferrous metal industry would be contained within a single classification called the "goods industry" and by this process of combining or aggregating these two industries under one system block they would lose their economic individuality.

The E-Model
A national economy consists of simultaneous flows of production, distribution, consumption, and investment. If all of these elements including labor and human functions are assigned a numerical value in like units of measure, say, 1939 dollars, then this flow can be further represented by a current flow in an electronic circuit, and its behavior can be predicted and manipulated with useful precision.

The three ideal passive energy components of electronics, the capacitor, the resistor, and the inductor correspond to the three ideal passive energy components of economics called the pure industries of capital, goods, and services, respectively.

- Economic capacitance represents the storage of capital in one form or another.
- Economic conductance represents the level of conductance of materials for the production of goods.
- Economic inductance represents the inertia of economic value in motion. This is a population phenomenon known as services.

Economic Inductance
An electrical inductor (e.g., a coil or wire) has an electric current as its primary phenomenon and a magnetic field as its secondary phenomenon (inertia). Corresponding to this, an economic inductor has a flow of economic value as its primary phenomenon and a population field as its secondary field phenomenon of inertia. When the flow of economic value (e.g., money) diminishes, the human population field collapses in order to keep the economic value (money) flowing (extreme case – war).

This public inertia is a result of consumer buying habits, expected standard of living, etc., and is generally a phenomenon of self-preservation.

Inductive Factors to Consider

1. Population
2. Magnitude of the economic activities of the government
3. The method of financing these government activities (See *Peter-Paul Principle* - inflation of the currency.)

Translation
(a few examples will be given.)

- Charge: coulombs; dollars (1939).
- Flow/Current: amperes (coulombs per second); dollars of flow per year.
- Motivating Force: volts; dollars (output) demand.
- Conductance: amperes per volt; dollars of flow per year per dollar demand.
- Capacitance: coulombs per volt; dollars of production inventory/stock per dollar demand.

Time Flow Relationships and Self-Destructive Oscillations
An ideal industry may be symbolized electronically in various ways. The simplest way is to represent a demand by a voltage and a supply by a current. When this is done, the relationship between the two becomes what is called an admittance, which can result from three economic factors: (1) foresight flow, (2) present flow, and (3) hindsight flow.

1. *Foresight flow* is the result of that property of living entities to cause energy (food) to be stored for a period of low energy (e.g., a winter season). It consists of demands made upon an economic system for that period of low energy (winter season).In a production industry it takes several forms, one of which is known as production stock or inventory. In electronic symbology this specific industry demand (a pure

capital industry) is represented by capacitance and the stock or resource is represented by a stored charge. Satisfaction of an industry demand suffers a lag because of the loading effect of inventory priorities.

2. *Present flow* ideally involves no delays. It is, so to speak, input today for output today, a "hand to mouth" flow. In electronic symbology, this specific industry demand (a pure us industry) is represented by a conductance which is then a simple economic valve (a dissipative element).

3. *Hindsight flow* is known as habit or inertia. In electronics this phenomenon is the characteristic of an inductor (economic analog = a pure service industry) in which a current flow (economic analog = flow of money) creates a magnetic field (economic analog = active human population) which, if the current (money flow) begins to diminish, collapse (war) to maintain the current (flow of money – energy). Other large alternatives to war as economic inductors or economic flywheels are an open-ended social welfare program, or an enormous (but fruitful) open-ended space program. The problem with stabilizing the economic system is that there is too much demand on account of (1) too much greed and (2) too much population. This creates excessive economic inductance which can only be balanced with economic capacitance (true resources or value – e.g., in goods or services). The social welfare program is nothing more than an open-ended credit balance system which creates a false capital industry to give nonproductive people a roof over their heads and food in their stomachs. This can be useful, however, because the recipients become state property in return for the "gift," a standing army for the elite. For he who pays the piper picks the tune. Those who get hooked on the economic drug, must go to the elite for a fix. In this, the method of introducing large amounts of stabilizing capacitance is by borrowing on the future "credit" of the world. This is a fourth law of motion – onset, and consists of performing an action and leaving the system before the reflected reaction returns to the point of action – a delayed reaction. The means of surviving the reaction is by changing the system before the reaction can return. By this means, politicians become more popular in their own time and the public pays later. In fact, the measure of such a politician is the delay time.

The same thing is achieved by a government by printing money beyond the limit of the gross national product, and economic process called *inflation*. This puts a large quantity of money into the hands of the public and maintains a balance against their greed, creates a false self-confidence in them and, for awhile, stays the wolf from the door.

They must eventually resort to war to balance the account, because war ultimately is merely the act of destroying the creditor, and the politicians are the publicly hired hit men that justify the act to keep the responsibility and blood off the public conscience. (See section on consent factors and social-economic structuring.)

If the people really cared about their fellow man, they would control their appetites (greed, procreation, etc.) so that they would not have to operate on a credit or welfare social system which steals from the worker to satisfy the bum.

Since most of the general public will not exercise restraint, there are only two alternatives to reduce the economic inductance of the system.

1. Let the populace bludgeon each other to death in war, which will only result in a total destruction of the living earth.

2. Take control of the world by the use of economic "silent weapons" in a form of "quiet warfare" and reduce the economic inductance of the world to a safe level by a process of benevolent slavery and genocide.

The latter option has been taken as the obviously better option. At this point it should be crystal clear to the reader why absolute secrecy about the silent weapons is necessary. The general public refuses to improve its own mentality and its faith in its fellow man. It has become a herd of proliferating barbarians, and, so to speak, a blight upon the face of the earth. They do not care enough about economic science to learn why they have not been able to avoid war despite religious morality, and their religious or self-gratifying refusal to deal with earthly problems renders the solution of the earthly problem unreachable to them.

It is left to those few who are truly willing to think and survive as the fittest to survive, to solve the problem for themselves as the few who really care. Otherwise, exposure of the silent weapon would destroy our only hope of preserving the seed of the future true humanity.

Industry Equivalent Circuits

The industry 'Q' can be given a block symbol as follows: Terminals #1 through #m are connected directly to the outputs of industries #1 and #m, respectively.

The equivalent circuit of industry 'Q' is given as follows:

Characteristics:

All inputs are at zero volts.

A – Amplifier – causes output current IQ to be represented by a voltage EQ. Amplifier delivers sufficient current at EQ to drive all loads Y10 through YmQ and sink all currents i1Q through imQ.

The unit transconductance amplifier AQ is constructed as follows:

* Arrow denotes the direction of the flow of capital, goods, and services. The total demand is given as EQ, where EQ=IQ.

The coupling network YPQ symbolizes the demand which industry Q makes on industry P. the connective admittance YPQ is called the 'technical coefficient' of the industry Q stating the demand of industry Q, called the industry of use, for the output in capital, goods, or services of industry P called the industry of origin.

The flow of commodities from industry P to industry Q is given by iPQ evaluated by the formula:

iPQ = YPQ* EQ. When the admittance YPQ is a simple conductance, this formula takes on the common appearance of Ohm's Law, iPQ = gPQ* IQ.The interconnection of a three industry system can be diagrammed as follows. The blocks of the industry diagram can be opened up revealing the technical coefficients, and a much simpler format. The equations of flow are given as follows:

Stages of Schematic Simplification

Generalization
All of this may now be summarized.
Let Ij represent the output of industry j, and

- ijk, the amount of the product of industry j absorbed annually by industry k, and
- ijo, the amount of the same product j made available for 'outside' use. Then

Substituting the technical coefficiences, yjk   which is the general equation of every admittance in the industry circuit.

Final Bill of Goods

is called the final bill of goods or the bill of final demand, and is zero when the system can be closed by the evaluation of the technical coefficients of the 'non-productive' industries, government and households. Households may be regarded as a productive industry with labor as its output product.

The Technical Coefficients
The quantities yjk are called the technical coefficients of the industrial system. They are admittances and can consist of any combination of three passive parameters, conductance, capacitance, and inductance. Diodes are used to make the flow unidirectional and point against the flow.

- gjk = economic conductance, absorption coefficient
- yjk = economic capacitance, capital coefficient
- Ljk = economic inductance, human activity coefficient

4.

1. **Types of Admittances**

The Household Industry
The industries of finance (banking), manufacturing, and government, real counterparts of the pure industries of capital, goods, and services, are easily defined because they are generally logically structured. Because of this their processes can be described mathematically and their technical coefficients can be easily deduced. This, however, is not the case with the service industry known as the household industry.

Household Models
When the industry flow diagram is represented by a 2-block system of households on the right and all other industries on the left, the

following results: The arrows from left to right labeled A, B, C, etc., denote flow of economic value from the industries in the left hand block to the industry in the right hand block called 'households'. These may be thought of as the monthly consumer flows of the following commodities. A -- alcoholic beverages, B – beef, C – coffee, ... , U – unknown, etc. . .
The problem which a theoretical economist faces is that the consumer preferences of any household is not easily predictable and the technical coefficients of any one household tend to be a nonlinear, very complex, and variable function of income, prices, etc.
Computer information derived from the use of the universal product code in conjuction with credit-card purchase as an individual household identifier could change this state of affairs, but the U.P.C. method is not yet available on a national or even a significant regional scale. To compensate for this data deficiency, an alternate indirect approach of analysis has been adopted known as economic shock testing. This method, widely used in the aircraft manufacturing industry, develops an aggregate statistical sort of data.

Applied to economics, this means that all of the households in one region or in the whole nation are studied as a group or class rather than individually, and the mass behavior rather than the individual behavior is used to discover useful estimates of the technical coefficients governing the economic structure of the hypothetical single-household industry.

Notice in the industry flow diagram that the values for the flows A, B, C, etc. are accessible to measurement in terms of selling prices and total sales of commodities.

One method of evaluating the technical coefficients of the household industry depends upon shocking the prices of a commodity and noting the changes in the sales of all of the commodities.

Economic Shock Testing

In recent times, the application of *Operations Research* to the study of the public economy has been obvious for anyone who understands the principles of shock testing.In the shock testing of an aircraft airframe, the recoil impulse of firing a gun mounted on that airframe causes shock waves in that structure which tell aviation engineers the conditions under which some parts of the airplane or the whole airplane or its wings will start to vibrate or flutter like a guitar string, a flute reed, or a tuning fork, and disintegrate or fall apart in flight.

Economic engineers achieve the same result in studying the behavior of the economy and the consumer public by carefully selecting a staple commodity such as beef, coffee, gasoline, or sugar, and then causing a sudden change or shock in its price or availability, thus kicking everybody's budget and buying habits out of shape.

They then observe the shock waves which result by monitoring the changes in advertising, prices, and sales of that and other commodities. The objective of such studies is to acquire the know-how to set the public economy into a predictable state of motion or change, even a controlled self-destructive state of motion which will convince the public that certain "expert" people should take control of the money system and reestablish security (rather than liberty and justice) for all. When the subject citizens are rendered unable to control their financial affairs, they, of course, become totally enslaved, a source of cheap labor.

Not only the prices of commodities, but also the availability of labor can be used as the means of shock testing. Labor strikes deliver excellent tests shocks to an economy, especially in the critical service areas of trucking (transportation), communication, public utilities (energy, water, garbage collection), etc.

By shock testing, it is found that there is a direct relationship between the availability of money flowing in an economy and the real psychological outlook and response of masses of people dependent upon that availability.

For example, there is a measurable quantitative relationship between the price of gasoline and the probability that a person would experience a headache, feel a need to watch a violent movie, smoke a cigarette, or go to a tavern for a mug of beer.

It is most interesting that, by observing and measuring the economic models by which the public tries to run from their problems and escape from reality, and by applying the mathematical theory of *Operations Research*, it is possible to program computers to predict the most probable combination of created events (shocks) which will bring about a complete control and subjugation of the public through a subversion of the public economy (by shaking the plum tree).

Introduction to the Theory of Economic Shock Testing

Let the prices and total sales of commodities be given and symbolized as follows:

Commodities	Price Function	Total Sales
alcoholic beverages	A	A
beef	B	B
coffee	C	C
gasoline	G	G
sugar	S	S
tobacco	T	T
unknown balance	U	U

Let us assume a simple economic model in which the total number of important (staple) commodities are represented as beef, gasoline, and an aggregate of all other staple commodities which we will call the hypothetical miscellaneous staple commodity 'M' (e.g., M is an aggregate of C, S, T, U, etc.).

Example of Shock Testing

Assume that the total sales, P, of petroleum products can be described by the linear function of the quantities B, G, and M, which are functions of the prices of those respective commodities.P = aPG B + aPG G + aPM MThen where B, G, and M are functions of the prices of beef, gasoline, and miscellaneous, respectively, and aPB, aPG, and aPM are constant coefficients defining the amount by which each of the functions B, G, and M affect the sales, P, of petroleum products. We are assuming that B, G, and M are variables independent of each other.

If the availability or price of gasoline is suddenly changed, then G must be replaced by G + Δ G. This causes a change in the

petroleum sales from P to P + Δ P. Also we will assume that B and M remain constant when G changes to G + Δ G.

(P + Δ P) = aPB B + aPG (G + Δ G) + aPMM.Expanding upon this expression, we get

P + Δ P = aPB B + aPG G + aPG Δ G + aPM M
and subtracting the original value of P we get for the change in P

Change in P = Δ P = aPG Δ G

Dividing by   G we get

aPG =   P /   G .

This is a rate of change in P due only to an isolated change in G,   G.

In general, ajk is the partial rate of change in the sales effect j due to a change in the causal price function of commodity k. If the interval of time were infinitesimal, this expression would be reduced to the definition of the total differential of a function, P.

When the price of gasoline is shocked, all of the coefficients with round G (2G) in the denominator are evaluated at the same time. If B, G, and M were independent, and sufficient for description of the economy, then three shock tests would be necessary to evaluate the system.

There are other factors which may be represented the same way.

For example, the tendency of a docile sub-nation to withdraw under economic pressure may be given by

where G is the price of gasoline, WP is the dollars spent per unit time (referenced to say 1939) for war production during 'peace'

time, etc. These quantities are presented to a computer in matrix format as follows:
and

X1 = GY1 = P – KPX2 = BY2 = F – KFX3 = etc.Y3 = etc.

Finally, inverting this matrix, i.e., solving for the Xk terms of the Yj, we get, say,

[bkj] [Yj] = [Xk] .This is the result into which we substitute to get that set of conditions of prices of commodities, bad news on TV, etc., which will deliver a collapse of public morale ripe for take over.

Once the economic price and sales coefficients ajk and bkj are determined, they may be translated into the technical supply and demand coefficients gjk, Cjk, and 1/Ljk.

Shock testing of a given commodity is then repeated to get the time rate of change of these technical coefficients.

Introduction to Economic Amplifiers

Economic amplifiers are the active components of economic engineering. The basic characteristic of any amplifier (mechanical, electrical, or economic) is that it receives an input control signal and delivers energy from an independent energy source to a specified output terminal in a predictable relationship to that input control signal.The simplest form of an economic amplifier is a device called advertising.

If a person is spoken to by a T.V. advertiser as if he were a twelve-year-old, then, due to suggestibility, he will, with a certain probability, respond or react to that suggestion with the uncritical response of a twelve-year-old and will reach into his economic reservoir and deliver its energy to but that product on impulse when he passes it in the store.

An economic amplifier may have several inputs and output. Its response might be instantaneous or delayed. Its circuit symbol might be a rotary switch if its options are exclusive, qualitative, "go" or "no-go", or it might have its parametric input/output relationships specified by a matrix with internal energy sources represented.

Whatever its form might be, its purpose is to govern the flow of energy from a source to an output sink in direct relationship to an input control signal. For this reason, it is called an active circuit element or component.

Economic Amplifiers fall into classes called strategies, and, in comparison with electronic amplifiers, the specific internal functions of an economic amplifier are called logistical instead of electrical.

Therefore, economic amplifiers not only deliver power gain but also, in effect, are used to cause changes in the economic circuitry.

In the design of an economic amplifier we must have some idea of at least five functions, which are:

1. the available input signals
2. the desired output-control objectives,
3. the strategic objective,
4. the available economic power sources,
5. the logistical options.

The process of defining and evaluating these factors and incorporating the economic amplifier into an economic system has been popularly called *game theory*.The design of an economic amplifier begins with a specification of the power level of the output, which can range from personal to national. The second condition is accuracy of response, i.e., how accurately the output action is a function of the input commands. High gain combined with strong feedback helps to deliver the required precision.

Most of the error will be in the input data signal. Personal input data tends to be specified, while national input data tends to be statistical.

Short List of Inputs

Questions to be answered:

- what
- where
- why
- when
- how
- who

General sources of information:

- telephone taps
- analysis of garbage
- surveillance
- behavior of children in school

Standard of living by:

- food
- shelter
- clothing
- transportation

Social contacts:

- telephone – itemized record of calls
- family – marriage certificates, birth certificates, etc.
- friends, associates, etc.
- memberships in organizations
- political affiliation

The Personal Paper Trail
Personal buying habits, i.e., personal consumer preferences:

- checking accounts
- credit-card purchases
- "tagged" credit-card purchases – the credit-card purchase of products bearing the U.P.C. (Universal Product Code)

Assets:

- checking accounts
- savings accounts
- real estate
- business
- automobile, etc.
- safety deposit at bank
- stock market

Liabilities:

- creditors
- enemies (see – legal)
- loans

Government sources (ploys)*:

- Welfare
- Social Security
- U.S.D.A. surplus food

- doles
- grants
- subsidies

* Principle of this ploy — the citizen will almost always make the collection of information easy if he can operate on the "free sandwich principle" of "eat now, and pay later."Government sources (via intimidation):

- Internal Revenue Service
- OSHA
- Census
- etc.

Other government sources — surveillance of U.S. mail.

Habit Patterns — Programming

Strengths and weaknesses:

- activities (sports, hobbies, etc.)
- see "legal" (fear, anger, etc. — crime record)
- hospital records (drug sensitivities, reaction to pain, etc.)
- psychiatric records (fears, angers, disgusts, adaptability, reactions to stimuli, violence, suggestibility or hypnosis, pain, pleasure, love, and sex)

Methods of coping — of adaptability — behavior:

- consumption of alcohol
- consumption of drugs
- entertainment
- religious factors influencing behavior
- other methods of escaping from reality

Payment modus operandi (MO) — pay on time, etc.:

- payment of telephone bills
- energy purchases
- water purchases
- repayment of loans
- house payments
- automobile payments
- payments on credit cards

Political sensitivity:

- beliefs
- contacts
- position
- strengths/weaknesses
- projects/activities

Legal inputs — behavioral control (Excuses for investigation, search, arrest, or employment of force to modify behavior)

- court records
- police records — NCIC
- driving record
- reports made to police
- insurance information
- anti-establishment acquaintances

- what
- where
- why
- when
- how
- who

General sources of information:

- telephone taps
- analysis of garbage
- surveillance
- behavior of children in school

Standard of living by:

- food
- shelter
- clothing
- transportation

Social contacts:

- telephone – itemized record of calls
- family – marriage certificates, birth certificates, etc.
- friends, associates, etc.
- memberships in organizations
- political affiliation

The Personal Paper Trail
Personal buying habits, i.e., personal consumer preferences:

- checking accounts
- credit-card purchases
- "tagged" credit-card purchases – the credit-card purchase of products bearing the U.P.C. (Universal Product Code)

Assets:

- checking accounts
- savings accounts
- real estate
- business
- automobile, etc.
- safety deposit at bank
- stock market

Liabilities:

- creditors
- enemies (see – legal)
- loans

Government sources (ploys)*:

- Welfare
- Social Security
- U.S.D.A. surplus food

- doles
- grants
- subsidies

* Principle of this ploy — the citizen will almost always make the collection of information easy if he can operate on the "free sandwich principle" of "eat now, and pay later."Government sources (via intimidation):

- Internal Revenue Service
- OSHA
- Census
- etc.

Other government sources — surveillance of U.S. mail.
Habit Patterns — Programming
Strengths and weaknesses:

- activities (sports, hobbies, etc.)
- see "legal" (fear, anger, etc. — crime record)
- hospital records (drug sensitivities, reaction to pain, etc.)
- psychiatric records (fears, angers, disgusts, adaptability, reactions to stimuli, violence, suggestibility or hypnosis, pain, pleasure, love, and sex)

Methods of coping — of adaptability — behavior:

- consumption of alcohol
- consumption of drugs
- entertainment
- religious factors influencing behavior
- other methods of escaping from reality

Payment modus operandi (MO) — pay on time, etc.:

- payment of telephone bills
- energy purchases
- water purchases
- repayment of loans
- house payments
- automobile payments
- payments on credit cards

Political sensitivity:

- beliefs
- contacts
- position
- strengths/weaknesses
- projects/activities

Legal inputs — behavioral control (Excuses for investigation, search, arrest, or employment of force to modify behavior)

- court records
- police records — NCIC
- driving record
- reports made to police
- insurance information
- anti-establishment acquaintances

National Input Information
Business sources (via I.R.S., etc):

- prices of commodities
- sales
- investments in
- stocks/inventory
- production tools and machinery
- buildings and improvements
- the stock market

Banks and credit bureaus:

- credit information
- payment information

Miscellaneous sources:

- polls and surveys
- publications
- telephone records
- energy and utility purchases

Short List of Outputs
Outputs — create controlled situations — manipulation of the economy, hence society — control by control of compensation and income.Sequence:

84. allocates opportunities.
85. destroys opportunities.
86. controls the economic environment.
87. controls the availability of raw materials.
88. controls capital.
89. controls bank rates.
90. controls the inflation of the currency.
91. controls the possession of property.
92. controls industrial capacity.
93. controls manufacturing.
94. controls the availability of goods (commodities).
95. controls the prices of commodities.
96. controls services, the labor force, etc.
97. controls payments to government officials.
98. controls the legal functions.
99. controls the personal data files — uncorrectable by the party slandered.
100. controls advertising.
101. controls media contact.
102. controls material available for T.V. viewing
103. disengages attention from real issues.
104. engages emotions.
105. creates disorder, chaos, and insanity.
106. controls design of more probing tax forms.
107. controls surveillance.
108. controls the storage of information.
109. develops psychological analyses and profiles of individuals.
110. controls legal functions [repeat of 15]
111. controls sociological factors.
112. controls health options.
113. preys on weakness.
114. cripples strengths.
115. leaches wealth and substance.

Table of Strategies

Do this:	To get this: Keep the public ignorant
Less public organization	Maintain access to control points for feedback
Required reaction to outputs (prices, sales)	
Create preoccupation	Lower defenses
Attack the family unit	Control of the education of the young
Give less cash and more credit and doles	More self-indulgence and more data
Attack the privacy of the church	Destroy faith in this sort of government
Social conformity	Computer programming simplicity
Minimize the tax protest	Maximum economic data, minimum enforcement problems
Stabilize the consent	Simplicity coefficients
Tighten control of variables	Simpler computer input data -- greater predictability
Establish boundary conditions	Problem simplicity / solutions of differential and difference equations
Proper timing	Less data shift and blurring
Maximize control	Minimum resistance to control
Collapse of currency	Destroy the faith of the American people in each other.

Diversion, the Primary Strategy

Experience has prevent that the simplest method of securing a silent weapon and gaining control of the public is to keep the public undisciplined and ignorant of the basic system principles on the one hand, while keeping them confused, disorganized, and distracted with matters of no real importance on the other hand. This is achieved by:

- disengaging their minds; sabotaging their mental activities; providing a low-quality program of public education in mathematics, logic, systems design and economics; and discouraging technical creativity.
- engaging their emotions, increasing their self-indulgence and their indulgence in emotional and physical activities, by:
- unrelenting emotional affrontations and attacks (mental and emotional rape) by way of constant barrage of sex, violence, and wars in the media – especially the T.V. and the newspapers.
- giving them what they desire – in excess – "junk food for thought" – and depriving them of what they really need.
- rewriting history and law and subjecting the public to the deviant creation, thus being able to shift their thinking from personal needs to highly fabricated outside priorities.

These preclude their interest in and discovery of the silent weapons of social automation technology. The general rule is that there is a profit in confusion; the more confusion, the more profit. Therefore, the best approach is to create problems and then offer solutions.

Diversion Summary

Media: Keep the adult public attention diverted away from the real social issues, and captivated by matters of no real importance. Schools: Keep the young public ignorant of real mathematics, real economics, real law, and real history.

Entertainment: Keep the public entertainment below a sixth-grade level.

Work: Keep the public busy, busy, busy, with no time to think; back on the farm with the other animals.

Consent, the Primary Victory

A silent weapon system operates upon data obtained from a docile public by legal (but not always lawful) force. Much information is made available to silent weapon systems programmers through the Internal Revenue Service. (See *Studies in the Structure of the American Economy* for an I.R.S. source list.) This information consists of the enforced delivery of well-organized data contained in federal and state tax forms, collected, assembled, and submitted by slave labor provided by taxpayers and employers.

Furthermore, the number of such forms submitted to the I.R.S. is a useful indicator of public consent, an important factor in strategic decision making. Other data sources are given in the Short List of Inputs.

Consent Coefficients – numerical feedback indicating victory status. Psychological basis: When the government is able to collect tax and seize private property without just compensation, it is an indication that the public is ripe for surrender and is consenting to enslavement and legal encroachment. A good and easily quantified indicator of harvest time is the number of public citizens who pay income tax despite an obvious lack of reciprocal or honest service from the government.

Amplification Energy Sources

The next step in the process of designing an economic amplifier is discovering the energy sources. The energy sources which support any primitive economic system are, of course, a supply of raw materials, and the consent of the people to labor and consequently assume a certain rank, position, level, or class in the social structure, i.e., to provide labor at various levels in the pecking order. Each class, in guaranteeing its own level of income, controls the class immediately below it, hence preserves the class structure. This provides stability and security, but also government from the top.

As time goes on and communication and education improve, the lower-class elements of the social labor structure become knowledgeable and envious of the good things that the upper-class members have. They also begin to attain a knowledge of energy systems and the ability to enforce their rise through the class structure.

This threatens the sovereignty of the elite.

If this rise of the lower classes can be postponed long enough, the elite can achieve energy dominance, and labor by consent no longer will hold a position of an essential energy source.

Until such energy dominance is absolutely established, the consent of people to labor and let others handle their affairs must be taken into consideration, since failure to do so could cause the people to interfere in the final transfer of energy sources to the control of the elite.

It is essential to recognize that at this time, public consent is still an essential key to the release of energy in the process of economic amplification.

Therefore, consent as an energy release mechanism will now be considered.

Logistics

The successful application of a strategy requires a careful study of inputs, outputs, the strategy connecting the inputs and the outputs, and the available energy sources to fuel the strategy. This study is called logistics.A logistical problem is studied at the elementary level first, and then levels of greater complexity are studied as a synthesis of elementary factors.

This means that a given system is analyzed, i.e., broken down into its subsystems, and these in turn are analyzed, until by this process, one arrives at the logistical "atom," the individual.

This is where the process of synthesis propery begins, at the time of birth of the individual.

The Artificial Womb

From the time a person leaves its mother's womb, its every effort is directed towards building, maintaining, and withdrawing into artificial wombs, various sorts of substitute protective devices or shells.The objective of these artificial wombs is to provide a stable environment for both stable and unstable activity; to provide a shelter for the evolutionary processes of growth and maturity – i.e., survival; to provide security for freedom and to provide defensive protection for offensive activity.

This is equally true of both the general public and the elite. However, there is a definite difference in the way each of these classes go about the solution of problems.

The Political Structure of a Nation – Dependency

The primary reason why the individual citizens of a country create a political structure is a subconscious wish or desire to perpetuate their own dependency relationship of childhood. Simply put, they want a human god to eliminate all risk from their life, pat them on the head, kiss their bruises, put a chicken on every dinner table, clothe their bodies, tuck them into bed at night, and tell them that everything will be alright when they wake up in the morning.This public demand is incredible, so the human god, the politician, meets incredibility with incredibility by promising the world and delivering nothing. So who is the bigger liar? the public? or the "godfather"?

This public behavior is surrender born of fear, laziness, and expediency. It is the basis of the welfare state as a strategic weapon, useful against a disgusting public.

Action/Offense

Most people want to be able to subdue and/or kill other human beings which disturb their daily lives, but they do not want to have to cope with the moral and religious issues which such an overt act on their part might raise. Therefore, they assign the dirty work to others (including their own children) so as to keep the blood off their hands. They rave about the humane treatment of animals and then sit down to a delicious hamburger from a whitewashed slaughterhouse down the street and out of sight. But even more hypocritical, they pay taxes to finance a professional association of hit men collectively called politicians, and then complain about corruption in government.

Responsibility

Again, most people want to be free to do the things (to explore, etc.) but they are afraid to fail.The fear of failure is manifested in irresponsibility, and especially in delegating those personal responsibilities to others where success is uncertain or carries possible or created liabilities (law) which the person is not prepared to accept. They want authority (root word – "author"), but they will not accept responsibility or liability. So they hire politicians to face reality for them.

Summary

The people hire the politicians so that the people can:

- obtain security without managing it.
- obtain action without thinking about it.
- inflict theft, injury, and death upon others without having to contemplate either life or death.
- avoid responsibility for their own intentions.
- obtain the benefits of reality and science without exerting themselves in the discipline of facing or learning either of these things.

They give the politicians the power to create and manage a war machine to:

- provide for the survival of the nation/womb.
- prevent encroachment of anything upon the nation/womb.
- destroy the enemy who threatens the nation/womb.
- destroy those citizens of their own country who do not conform for the sake of stability of the nation/womb.

Politicians hold many quasi-military jobs, the lowest being the police which are soldiers, the attorneys and C.P.A.s next who are spies and saboteurs (licensed), and the judges who shout orders and run the closed union military shop for whatever the market will bear. The generals are industrialists. The "presidential" level of commander-in-chief is shared by the international bankers. The people know that they have created this farce and financed it with their own taxes (consent), but they would rather knuckle under than be the hypocrite.Thus, a nation becomes divided into two very distinct parts, a docile sub-nation [great silent majority] and a political sub-nation. The political sub-nation remains attached to the docile sub-nation, tolerates it, and leaches its substance until it grows strong enough to detach itself and then devour its parent.

System Analysis

In order to make meaningful computerized economic decisions about war, the primary economic flywheel, it is necessary to assign concrete logistical values to each element of the war structure – personnel and material alike.This process begins with a clear and candid description of the subsystems of such a structure.

The Draft (As military service)

Few efforts of human behavior modification are more remarkable or more effective than that of the socio-military institution known as the draft. A primary purpose of a draft or other such institution is to instill, by intimidation, in the young males of a society the uncritical conviction that the government is omnipotent. He is soon taught that a prayer is slow to reverse what a bullet can do in an instant. Thus, a man trained in a religious environment for eighteen years of his life can, by this instrument of the government, be broken down, be purged of his fantasies and delusions in a matter of mere months. Once that conviction is instilled, all else becomes easy to instill.Even more interesting is the process by which a young man's parents, who purportedly love him, can be induced to send him off to war to his death. Although the scope of this work will not allow this matter to be expanded in full detail, nevertheless, a coarse overview will be possible and can serve to reveal those factors which must be included in some numerical form in a computer analysis of social and war systems. We begin with a tentative definition of the draft.

2.   The draft (selective service, etc.) is an institution of compulsory collective sacrifice and slavery, devised by the middle-aged and elderly for the purpose of pressing the young into doing the public dirty work. It further serves to make the youth as guilty as the elders, thus making criticism of the elders by the youth less likely (Generational Stabilizer). It is marketed and and sold to the public under the label of "patriotic = national" service.Once a candid economic definition of the draft is achieved, that definition is used to outline the boundaries of a structure called a Human Value System, which in turn is translated into the terms of game theory. The value of such a slave laborer is given in a Table of Human Values, a table broken down into categories by intellect, experience, post-service job demand, etc.Some of these categories are ordinary and can be tentatively evaluated in terms of the value of certain jobs for which a known fee exists. Some jobs are harder to value because they are unique to the demands of social subversion, for an extreme example: the value of a mother's instruction to her daughter, causing that daughter to put certain behavioral demands upon a future husband ten or fifteen years hence; thus, by suppressing his resistance to a perversion of a government, making it easier for a banking cartel to buy the State of New York in, say, twenty years.Such a problem leans heavily upon the observations and data of wartime espionage and many types of psychological testing. But crude mathematical models (algorithms, etc.) can be devised, if not to predict, at least to predeterminate these events with maximum certainty. What does not exist by natural cooperation is thus enhanced by calculated compulsion. Human beings are machines, levers which may be grasped and turned, and there is little real difference between automating a society and automating a shoe factory.These derived values are variable. (It is necessary to use a current Table of Human Values for computer analysis.) These values are given in true measure rather than U.S. dollars, since the latter is unstable, being presently inflated beyond the production of national goods and services so as to give the economy a false kinetic energy ("paper" inductance).The silver value is stable, it being possible to buy the same amount with a gram of silver today as it could be bought in 1920. Human value measured in silver units changes slightly due to changes in production technology.

Enforcement

Factor IAs in every social system approach, stability is achieved only by understanding and accounting for human nature (action/reaction patterns). A failure to do so can be, and usually is, disastrous.As in other human social schemes, one form or another of intimidation (or incentive) is essential to the success of the draft. Physical principles of action and reaction must be applied to both internal and external subsystems.To secure the draft, individual brainwashing/programming and both the family unit and the peer group must be engaged and brought under control.Factor II – FatherThe man of the household must be housebroken to ensure that junior will grow up with the right social training and attitudes. The advertising media, etc., are engaged to see to it that father-to-be is pussy-whipped before or by the time he is married. He is taught that he either conforms to the social notch cut out for him or his sex life will be hobbled and his tender companionship will be zero. He is made to see that women demand security more than logical, principled, or honorable behavior.By the time his son must go to war, father (with jelly for a backbone) will slam a gun into junior's hand before father will risk the censure of his peers, or make a hypocrite of himself by crossing the investment he has in his own personal opinion or self-esteem. Junior will go to war or father will be embarrassed. So junior will go to war, the true purpose not withstanding.Factor III – MotherThe female element of human society is ruled by emotion first and logic second. In the battle between logic and imagination, imagination always wins, fantasy prevails, maternal instinct dominates so that the child comes first and the future comes second. A woman with a newborn baby is too starry-eyed to see a wealthy man's cannon fodder or a cheap source of slave labor. A woman must, however, be conditioned to accept the transition to "reality" when it comes, or sooner.As the transition becomes more difficult to manage, the family unit must be carefully disintegrated, and state-controlled public education and state-operated child-care centers must be become more common and legally enforced so as to begin the detachment of the child from the mother and father at an earlier age. Inoculation of behavioral drugs [Ritalin] can speed the transition for the child (mandatory). Caution: A woman's impulsive anger can override her fear. An irate woman's power must never be underestimated, and her power over a pussy-whipped husband must likewise never be underestimated. It got women the vote in 1920.Factor IV – JuniorThe emotional pressure for self-preservation during the time of war and the self-serving attitude of the common herd that have an option to avoid the battlefield – if junior can be persuaded to go – is all of the pressure finally necessary to propel Johnny off to war. Their quiet blackmailings of him are the threats: "No sacrifice, no friends; no glory, no girlfriends."Factor V – SisterAnd what about junior's sister? She is given all the good things of life by her father, and taught to expect the same from her future husband regardless of the price.Factor VI – CattleThose who will not use their brains are no better off than those who have no brains, and so this mindless school of jelly-fish, father, mother, son, and daughter, become useful beasts of burden or trainers of the same.

This concludes what is available of this document.